SPIRITUALITY

GUIDANCE FOR A
BETTER LIFE

SOPHIE GOLDING

SPIRITUALITY

An Hachette UK Company
www.hachette.co.uk

Vie Books, an imprint of Summersdale Publishers Ltd
Part of Octopus Publishing Group Limited
Carmelite House
50 Victoria Embankment
LONDON
EC4Y 0DZ
UK

www.summersdale.com

Printed and bound in China

ISBN: 978-1-78685-969-3

Substantial discounts on bulk quantities of Summersdale books are available to corporations, professional associations and other organizations. For details contact general enquiries: telephone: +44 (0) 1243 771107 or email: enquiries@summersdale.com.

Contents

Introduction 4

Part 1: Everyday Spirituality 6

Part 2: Spirituality Practices 45

Part 3: Spiritual Development 112

Part 4: Faith and Religions 146

Conclusion 191

INTRODUCTION

The benefits of embracing a spiritual lifestyle are enormous. A spiritual lifestyle will bring you peace and happiness; it will teach you how to handle difficult situations with a calm and considered approach; it will help you to discover what is truly important to you and give you the confidence to reach your goals. You will no longer regard challenges as obstacles and you will come to understand that the answers you seek are already within you.

This book shows you how to start your spiritual journey, drawing together wisdom from the world's greatest traditions that has guided and inspired people for centuries. By exploring the different ideas and philosophies within this world, you will discover which principles ring true for you. There are also practical tips and techniques for you to try, which will help you to incorporate spirituality into your everyday life, discover new ways of thinking and increase your self-awareness.

Setting aside a little time to try out these simple techniques will bring you huge rewards, from your new attitude of positivity and compassion through to a greater connection with your spiritual self and the world around you. You'll live a happier, healthier and more authentic life, which is the best reward of all.

PART 1

Everyday Spirituality

GET TO KNOW YOUR SPIRITUAL SELF

Spirituality is a personal journey whereby we try to establish and nurture a connection with something greater than ourselves. To do this, we must first look to ourselves: at our beliefs, our values and our actions. What could you change or improve upon? Based on your life to date, create an honest personal inventory of yourself. Explore your character traits, ideals and beliefs, paying particular attention to the themes of fairness, honesty and love, and acknowledge your strengths as well as your weaknesses.

The following questions will help you discover your core values and create your inventory:

- What are my positive and negative qualities?
- Do I have a belief system?
- Are there outstanding apologies or amends I need to make that would give me greater peace of mind? If there are but this is not possible, can I forgive myself and move on knowing that I will not repeat this behaviour?
- What resentments am I carrying that it would do me good to let go of?

A truthful moral inventory provides a sound basis from which to begin your journey to enlightenment and will help you tune into a more spiritual mindset.

Knowing yourself is the beginning of all wisdom.

Aristotle

A journey of a thousand miles begins with a single step.

Lao Tzu

THINK POSITIVE

Emotional health and spiritual balance require a positive state of mind, so cultivate a "can do" mindset until this becomes instinctive. Practising positivity, especially towards others, diminishes negative emotions such as hate, envy and jealousy and leaves your mind and heart clearer and lighter. Be willing and ready to seek out silver linings even in the darkest of situations.

Make a conscious decision to be on the lookout for negative thoughts and be ready to challenge them whenever they pop into your head. If they do, try a mindfulness exercise, such as visualizing your negativity being carried away on the breeze and out of your sight.

Choose your company wisely: if you know someone to be a doomsayer who always steals your sunshine, give them a wide berth. Or be prepared to call them out on their habit of always seeing the glass as half empty. People can only drain your positivity if you allow them to.

in every day,
there are

1,440

minutes.
that means
we have

1,440

daily opportunities
to make a
positive impact.

Les Brown

What
you need
is to recognize
the possibilities and
challenges offered by
the present moment, and
to embrace them.

Thomas Merton

START AS YOU MEAN TO GO ON

Start every day with a moment of reflection.
Even if you don't pray or meditate, a
short time spent focusing on how
you intend to face the day ahead can bring
great clarity and set you up to achieve
your goals and objectives. Aim to be the
best possible version of yourself.

MAKE
EACH DAY
YOUR
MASTERPIECE.

John Wooden

CREATE ORDER FROM CHAOS

It is almost impossible to feel a spiritual connection to anything if you are living in chaos. If you have a tendency to create mess, make a concerted effort to be neater: put things away, clean up after yourself as you go, and keep on top of domestic chores. A tidy environment is reflective of your inner self: tidy home, tidy mind. There is something soothing and rhythmic about tidying and cleaning, so the act itself can be beneficial to our spiritual health and sense of contentment.

Life has a way of setting things
in order and leaving them be.

Very tidy, is life.

Jean Anouilh

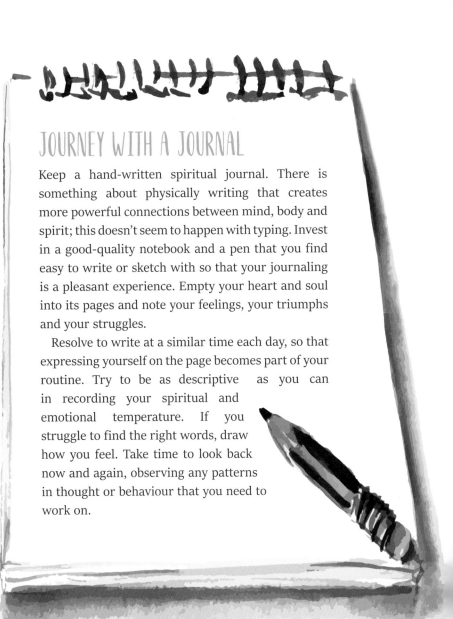

JOURNEY WITH A JOURNAL

Keep a hand-written spiritual journal. There is something about physically writing that creates more powerful connections between mind, body and spirit; this doesn't seem to happen with typing. Invest in a good-quality notebook and a pen that you find easy to write or sketch with so that your journaling is a pleasant experience. Empty your heart and soul into its pages and note your feelings, your triumphs and your struggles.

Resolve to write at a similar time each day, so that expressing yourself on the page becomes part of your routine. Try to be as descriptive   as you can in recording your spiritual and emotional temperature. If you struggle to find the right words, draw how you feel. Take time to look back now and again, observing any patterns in thought or behaviour that you need to work on.

Writing in a journal offers a place where you can hold a deliberate, thoughtful conversation with yourself.

Robin Sharma

DIGITAL DETOX

Although technology is an integral part of daily life, try to find time every day (or at least once a week) when you can detach from all digital paraphernalia. Switch off your phone and all other devices and relish the freedom it brings. Reducing our interaction with the digital world reduces stress and enables us to step back to re-evaluate, refocus and reconnect with loved ones. Instead of frittering an hour away on social media, do something unrelated to technology that you enjoy but haven't done for ages. Do what you love instead of looking for "likes".

Bedtime is a good daily point to disconnect. The light from screens reduces production of melatonin, which is one of the hormones that helps us get to sleep, so turn off devices at least two hours before you go to bed and make your bedroom a tech-free zone. Instead of reading emails, read an inspirational book or practise mindfulness. At least twice a year, take a digital detox holiday. Even a long weekend without logging on will help clear your head and improve your connection with the cosmos.

Radiate peace.
Who knows? The peace
you spread may create
the only restful place in
your environment.

Stella Payton

Be the calm centre in the raging flow of life.

Leo Babauta

STARTING OVER

It's easy to let something
upsetting dictate your mood
or attitude for the rest of the
day. When this happens, get
into the habit of beginning
your day again and make a
conscious decision to return
to a place of calm. Even if it is
last thing at night, say out loud
"I am starting my day again",
and reclaim your equilibrium.

YESTERDAY IS THE PAST, TOMORROW IS THE FUTURE, BUT TODAY IS A GIFT. THAT IS WHY IT IS CALLED THE PRESENT.

Bil Keane

ANIMAL TRANQUILLITY

Spending time with animals can have a profoundly calming effect. Time with animals is often used to help rehabilitate people suffering from depression and nervous afflictions. Try volunteering at a local sanctuary, taking a friend's dog on a long walk or stroking a cat while it is sitting on your lap. It is almost impossible to feel anything other than peaceful contentment when you have a feline friend purring away on your knees.

Until one has loved an animal, a part of one's soul remains unawakened.

Anatole France

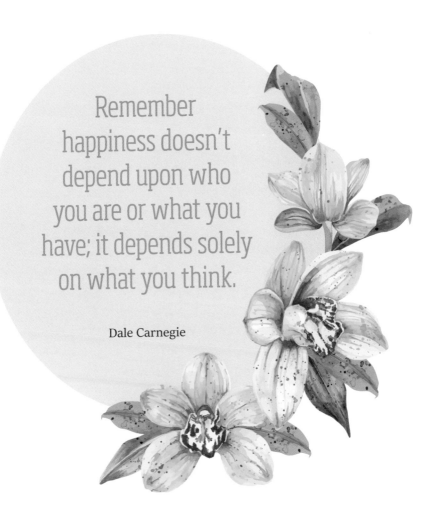

Remember happiness doesn't depend upon who you are or what you have; it depends solely on what you think.

Dale Carnegie

GO BACK TO YOUR ROOTS

Take a trip down memory lane and discover your ancestors. People from many cultures and spiritual traditions from around the world venerate their ancestors as an important part of their identity. By looking back at where we came from, we can get a better grasp on who we are, what we stand for and where our place is in the world. We all long to "belong", and discovering the extent of our family trees can be a spiritual experience. Who knows? You might unearth a famous relative, or learn that you may have inherited talents for things you never thought to try.

Talk to grandparents and older relatives about the life and work of your forebears. Ask them to talk you through photograph albums and to share their memories. If there are particularly fascinating stories to be told, take advantage of the digital age and record them – to inspire you and the generations to come.

You may want to set aside a corner of your home where you can display pictures of your ancestors, light a candle to remember them or add a vase of flowers as a token of gratitude for the gifts they have passed down to you.

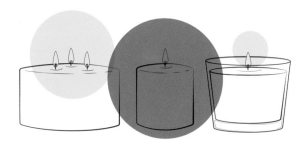

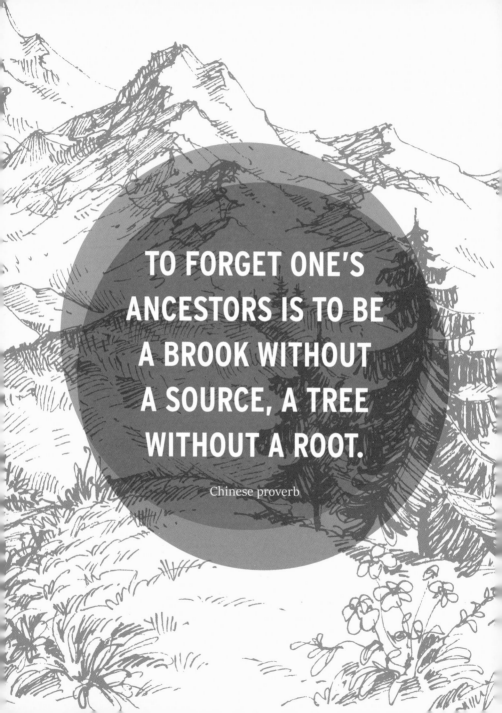

TO FORGET ONE'S
ANCESTORS IS TO BE
A BROOK WITHOUT
A SOURCE, A TREE
WITHOUT A ROOT.

Chinese proverb

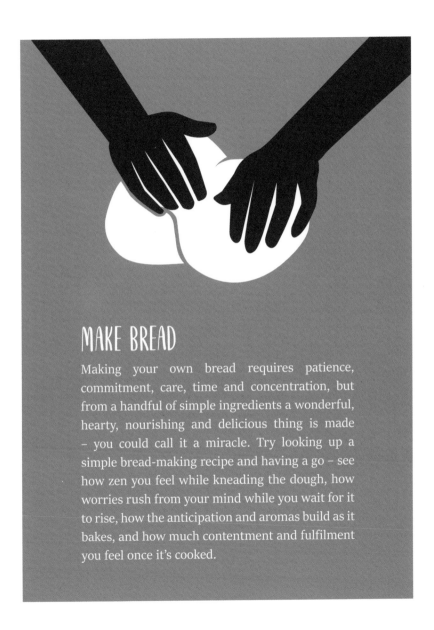

MAKE BREAD

Making your own bread requires patience, commitment, care, time and concentration, but from a handful of simple ingredients a wonderful, hearty, nourishing and delicious thing is made – you could call it a miracle. Try looking up a simple bread-making recipe and having a go – see how zen you feel while kneading the dough, how worries rush from your mind while you wait for it to rise, how the anticipation and aromas build as it bakes, and how much contentment and fulfilment you feel once it's cooked.

INSIGHT OCCURS WHEN, AND TO THE DEGREE THAT, ONE KNOWS ONESELF.

Andrew Schneider

EVERYDAY ENLIGHTENMENT

Try incorporating the quest for enlightenment into your daily life by making use of the numerous podcasts available on a whole range of subjects connected to spirituality. From religious services to inspirational talks and speeches, there's something out there for all tastes.

If you spend a lot of time travelling on public transport, there are various apps you can use to advance your enlightenment. Alternatively, you could make use of the multitude of books available on all things spiritual. You may be stuck in a tunnel on the 6:15 to Waterloo, but while you're there you may as well be keeping your aura in tip-top condition or learning more about ancient sages and their timeless wisdom.

Just as a candle
cannot burn
without fire,
man cannot
live without a
spiritual life.

Buddhist proverb

HEAL WITH HERBS

Plant herbs in a pot to keep around the house or in the garden. Fresh herbs bring you into direct contact with nature, which is the first step to finding physical and spiritual balance. Herbs are well known for their medicinal uses too: check reputable resources online or find a book on herbal remedies by an acknowledged expert and you'll have access to centuries-old wisdom on treating virtually any ailment.

THE ART OF HEALING
COMES FROM NATURE,
NOT FROM THE PHYSICIAN.
THEREFORE THE PHYSICIAN
MUST START FROM NATURE,
WITH AN OPEN MIND.

Paracelsus

CREATIVITY FOR THE SOUL

Whether it's painting a picture, colouring in, writing a poem, embroidering a cushion cover or weaving with willow, tapping into an art, craft or otherwise, creative activity is good for the soul. It doesn't matter how accomplished you are; the very act of creating something is positive. Especially good for alleviating acute anxiety and obsessional thoughts, getting arty or crafty is a wonderful way to distract yourself and find a more composed state of mind.

CALM WITH COLOUR

By learning to celebrate your senses – smell,
touch, sight, hearing and taste – you'll give your
brain a well-earned rest from multi-tasking.
Many people find that becoming absorbed in a
creative pursuit, such as colouring, can help them
to focus in this way. To get you started, there are
plenty of books and apps available that combine
colouring with gentle mindfulness exercises.

Creativity takes COURAGE.

Henri Matisse

ART ENABLES US TO FIND OURSELVES AND LOSE OURSELVES AT THE SAME TIME.

Thomas Merton

SING OUT LOUD

Singing is proven to move our focus away from everyday concerns and towards something more spiritual. It unites people and creates positive energy, all the while soothing bodily systems and activating our natural healing processes. Moreover, it is a way of expressing your soul. Try singing to yourself as you do housework, or consider joining a choir.

DANCE AND SING IT OUT

Bring music into your life and joy will come
with it. Dance, sing and laugh as often as
you possibly can. Remember what it was
like to be a child, when unselfconsciousness
and spontaneity ruled. Sometimes, as adults,
we are afraid to show or feel happiness.
Aspire to express yourself through music.

MUSIC AND SPIRITUALITY

Keening, incantations, requiems, hymns, classical scores and modern music have all been used to express and enrich spiritual occasions. Make a playlist of music to inspire you when you are struggling to make a spiritual connection. Tap into pieces that touch you on a profound level. Don't limit yourself to any one genre – if you find folk songs, musicals or even the theme tunes to TV shows spiritually awakening, turn up the volume and let the music play on.

We are the music makers, And we are the dreamers of dreams.

Arthur O'Shaughnessy

PART 2
Spirituality Practices

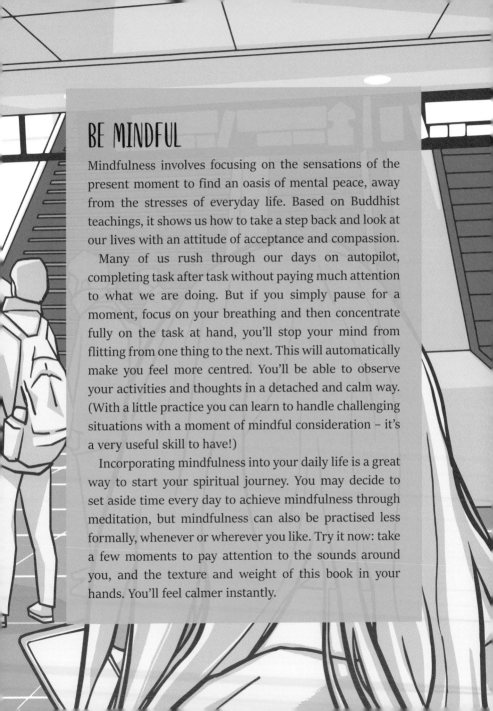

BE MINDFUL

Mindfulness involves focusing on the sensations of the present moment to find an oasis of mental peace, away from the stresses of everyday life. Based on Buddhist teachings, it shows us how to take a step back and look at our lives with an attitude of acceptance and compassion.

Many of us rush through our days on autopilot, completing task after task without paying much attention to what we are doing. But if you simply pause for a moment, focus on your breathing and then concentrate fully on the task at hand, you'll stop your mind from flitting from one thing to the next. This will automatically make you feel more centred. You'll be able to observe your activities and thoughts in a detached and calm way. (With a little practice you can learn to handle challenging situations with a moment of mindful consideration – it's a very useful skill to have!)

Incorporating mindfulness into your daily life is a great way to start your spiritual journey. You may decide to set aside time every day to achieve mindfulness through meditation, but mindfulness can also be practised less formally, whenever or wherever you like. Try it now: take a few moments to pay attention to the sounds around you, and the texture and weight of this book in your hands. You'll feel calmer instantly.

There's no past
and there's
no future.
All there is,
ever,
is the now.

George Harrison

DON'T LOOK BACK AND ASK, WHY? LOOK AHEAD AND ASK, WHY NOT?

Neil Patel

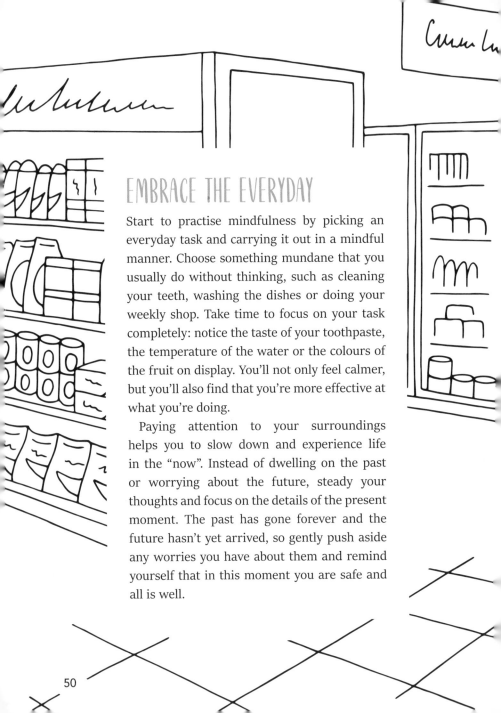

EMBRACE THE EVERYDAY

Start to practise mindfulness by picking an everyday task and carrying it out in a mindful manner. Choose something mundane that you usually do without thinking, such as cleaning your teeth, washing the dishes or doing your weekly shop. Take time to focus on your task completely: notice the taste of your toothpaste, the temperature of the water or the colours of the fruit on display. You'll not only feel calmer, but you'll also find that you're more effective at what you're doing.

Paying attention to your surroundings helps you to slow down and experience life in the "now". Instead of dwelling on the past or worrying about the future, steady your thoughts and focus on the details of the present moment. The past has gone forever and the future hasn't yet arrived, so gently push aside any worries you have about them and remind yourself that in this moment you are safe and all is well.

THE PURSUIT, EVEN OF THE BEST THINGS, OUGHT TO BE CALM AND TRANQUIL.

Marcus Tullius Cicero

YOGA IS A LIGHT,
WHICH ONCE LIT,
WILL NEVER DIM.
THE BETTER YOU PRACTISE,
THE BRIGHTER THE FLAME.

B. K. S. Iyengar

TRY YOGA

Yoga is a Sanskrit word meaning "to join or unite". It generally refers to the union between soul and body, and is a practice that can form part of any belief system, although it has its roots in Hindu teachings. Many of us in the Western world are familiar with yoga as a form of physical exercise, but it has a deeply spiritual element too. It is a holistic system, balancing the mind, body and spirit.

Stretching the mind as well as the muscles, yoga is a wonderful way to relax and to quieten the soul. It centres us in the present and enables us to be more aware of our higher consciousness. Studies have also shown that regular "yogis" are more adept at soothing their nervous systems and find it easier to connect with their spiritual selves. The regular practice of yoga can also lead to physical benefits, such as improved heart health, greater flexibility and better posture, while also enhancing your spiritual and mental well-being.

Hatha (or active) yoga is the most common type practised in the West. It combines various strengthening postures and stretches with breathing and meditation exercises, and its benefits include increased flexibility and relaxation, as well as relief from stress and pain. There are many different styles of hatha yoga, with different emphases on posture, meditation and yogic breathing.

Making yoga a part of your daily routine – even if it's something as simple as a relaxation exercise – will increase your mindfulness and enhance your well-being.

FIND A GURU

Whether you track down a local class or try out some one-to-one lessons, getting guidance from someone you trust is the best place to start. In life we often feel that it's down to us to solve everything ourselves, but learning to take advice from others is a good skill to develop. Many qualities we cultivate in yoga, such as balance, concentration and perseverance, are useful in other areas of our lives, too.

PRACTISE A POSE

Practise the tree pose daily to improve your strength, coordination and concentration. Stand with your arms at your sides and then transfer your weight to one foot, lift the sole of your other foot and press it firmly into your balancing leg. (The goal is to get your foot onto your opposite thigh, but if this is too challenging, aim lower and place your foot just above the ankle.) Hold for 30 seconds and then repeat with the other leg.

RELAX AND RELEASE

Most yoga classes finish with a relaxation exercise. Try this after a stressful day: lie on your back with your arms stretched out by your sides. Close your eyes and breathe slowly and deeply. Focus on relaxing each part of your body in turn, from your head down to your feet. At each stage, release any tension and imagine yourself sinking into the floor beneath you. Finish by gently moving your fingers and toes before opening your eyes.

Exercises are like prose,

whereas yoga is the

poetry of movements.

Amit Ray

YOGIC BREATHING

Yogic breathing, or pranayama, lies at the heart of yoga practice. Defined as the control of life force, yogic breathing increases vital energy in the body, and calms and steadies the mind. Other benefits include improved digestion and sleep. Since focusing on breathing helps us to achieve mindfulness, yogic breathing is also a route to all the benefits of mindfulness and meditation.

There are many different yogic breathing techniques, each with a different focus, but making any effort to deepen your breathing will be beneficial, as you'll be providing your body with a better supply of oxygen. Most of us rarely think about the way we breathe and use only 50 per cent of our lung capacity, snatching shallow breaths into the top of our lungs. Practise breathing from the diaphragm whenever you can and you'll feel instantly re-energized.

Sit in a comfortable position with your shoulders slightly back to open up your chest. Placing your hand on your stomach, exhale through the mouth and inhale deeply and slowly through the nose, feeling your hand rise and fall with each breath. Once you've mastered this simple exercise and felt the benefits, you can move on to explore different breathing techniques (for cleansing, relaxation, combatting stress, etc.). Internet tutorials are excellent for this – you can even fit a little yogic breathing into your lunch break.

That's why it's called a practice. We have to practise a practice if it is to be of value.

Allan Lokos

BE WITH TREES

Trees are said to be rich in mystical and natural energy. Studies have confirmed that walking among trees and even hugging them can help in the treatment of depression and anxiety; so if you are feeling blue, pull on your boots and make a pilgrimage to your favourite forested area. You could try forest bathing (Shinrin-yoku), which was developed in Japan in the 1980s as a preventative medicine. Patients report improvements to their sense of well-being and calm from simply spending time in the forest.

Pagans set great store in the properties of different varieties of tree and believe that each species can confer its own unique benefits. For instance, if you are seeking emotional stability, sit beneath a willow; if you need strength, embrace an oak tree. A birch tree is said to represent new beginnings, while a stint in the company of a holly tree will help alleviate anger. If romance is on your mind, daydream beneath a blossoming cherry tree.

Trees are poems that the earth writes upon the sky.

Kahlil Gibran

IN A
FOREST OF
A HUNDRED
THOUSAND
TREES, NO TWO
LEAVES ARE ALIKE,
JUST AS NO TWO
JOURNEYS ALONG
THE SAME PATH
ARE THE SAME.

Paulo Coelho

SENSORY STROLLING

Balm to the soul, a sensory walk by the sea, in
the woods, mountains or countryside, or in peaceful
parkland, frees the mind, exercises the body and puts
our senses through their paces. Decide on a location,
make sure you're dressed for the weather and walk with
the express purpose of utilizing all of your senses.
Really see, hear and smell your surroundings: what do you
notice? What colours delight your eyes? How many sounds can
you identify? Stick your tongue out and see if you can taste,
say, the salt from the sea. Touch the natural world: run
sand, grass, earth or lake water through your fingers
and stroke flower petals and tree bark. Pay attention
to the different textures. Invigorating and
centring, a sensory walk is both
inspiring and restorative.

The POETRY OF eaRth iS NeVeR Dead.

John Keats

THE MOUNTAINS ARE CALLING AND I MUST GO.

John Muir

PILGRIM'S PROGRESS

If there is somewhere that you feel a spiritual connection to, and it's close enough for you to visit, make a pilgrimage. A beach, a landmark, a building – make time to visit and allow your spiritual energy to flow. If there is somewhere further afield that you have always felt a "pull" towards, follow your instinct and consider saving for a short break or holiday there.

Most people agree that even if you aren't religious, being in a temple, mosque or church is a peaceful experience. Visit a religious building and simply sit and enjoy the surroundings and the tranquillity. Meditate or just absorb the quietude. You don't need to participate in a religious tradition to appreciate its rituals and places of worship.

I like the silent church before the service begins, better than any preaching.

Ralph Waldo Emerson

Happiness is *spiritual,* born of *truth & love.* It is *unselfish;* therefore it cannot *exist alone,* but requires all mankind to *share it.*

Mary Baker Eddy

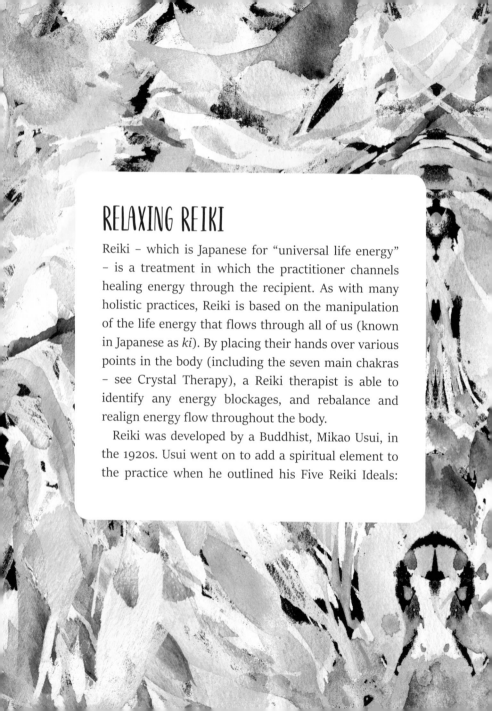

RELAXING REIKI

Reiki – which is Japanese for "universal life energy" – is a treatment in which the practitioner channels healing energy through the recipient. As with many holistic practices, Reiki is based on the manipulation of the life energy that flows through all of us (known in Japanese as *ki*). By placing their hands over various points in the body (including the seven main chakras – see Crystal Therapy), a Reiki therapist is able to identify any energy blockages, and rebalance and realign energy flow throughout the body.

Reiki was developed by a Buddhist, Mikao Usui, in the 1920s. Usui went on to add a spiritual element to the practice when he outlined his Five Reiki Ideals:

do not anger; do not worry; be filled with gratitude; devote yourself to your work; and be kind to others. Usui felt that it was important for Reiki recipients to take responsibility for their own spiritual healing by resolving to improve themselves in this way.

Reiki is a relaxing, non-intrusive treatment. Some people feel sensations of tingling or heat during a session. They may experience an emotional reaction too, as the chakras are rebalanced. The best way to benefit from Reiki is to try a taster session (these are often available at holistic fairs) or check online to find a therapist. You can also be taught to practise Reiki yourself – a weekend course is enough to get you started at a basic level, allowing self-treatment. It is an excellent way to de-stress, and achieve physical and emotional balance.

REIKI IS LOVE, LOVE IS WHOLENESS, WHOLENESS IS BALANCE,

BALANCE IS WELL-BEING, WELL-BEING IS FREEDOM FROM DISEASE.

Mikao Usui

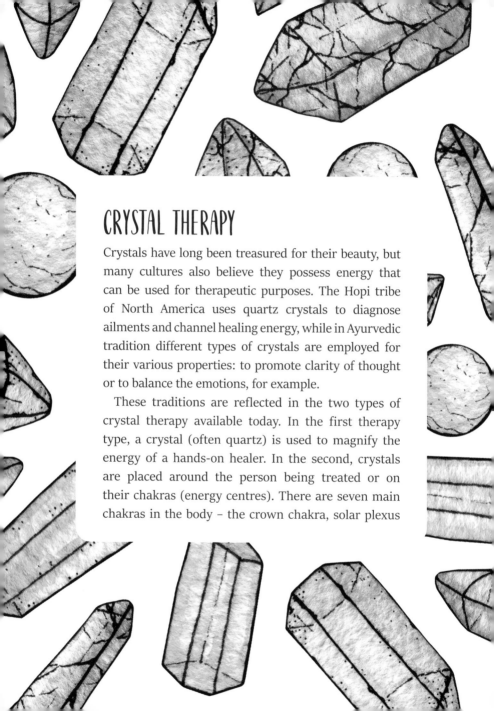

CRYSTAL THERAPY

Crystals have long been treasured for their beauty, but many cultures also believe they possess energy that can be used for therapeutic purposes. The Hopi tribe of North America uses quartz crystals to diagnose ailments and channel healing energy, while in Ayurvedic tradition different types of crystals are employed for their various properties: to promote clarity of thought or to balance the emotions, for example.

These traditions are reflected in the two types of crystal therapy available today. In the first therapy type, a crystal (often quartz) is used to magnify the energy of a hands-on healer. In the second, crystals are placed around the person being treated or on their chakras (energy centres). There are seven main chakras in the body – the crown chakra, solar plexus

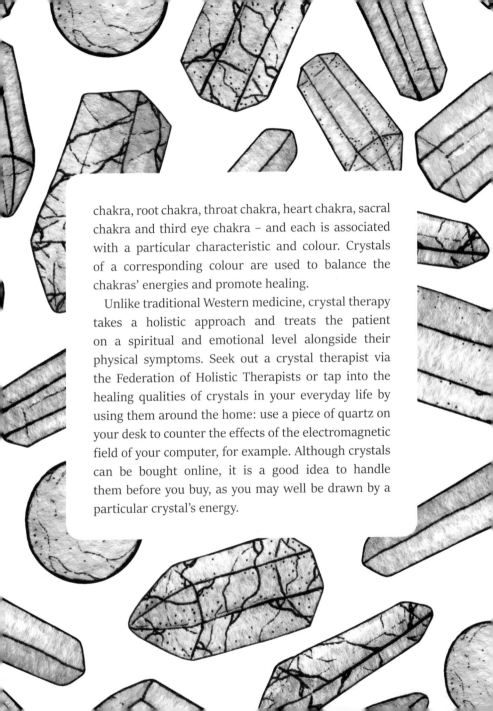

chakra, root chakra, throat chakra, heart chakra, sacral chakra and third eye chakra – and each is associated with a particular characteristic and colour. Crystals of a corresponding colour are used to balance the chakras' energies and promote healing.

Unlike traditional Western medicine, crystal therapy takes a holistic approach and treats the patient on a spiritual and emotional level alongside their physical symptoms. Seek out a crystal therapist via the Federation of Holistic Therapists or tap into the healing qualities of crystals in your everyday life by using them around the home: use a piece of quartz on your desk to counter the effects of the electromagnetic field of your computer, for example. Although crystals can be bought online, it is a good idea to handle them before you buy, as you may well be drawn by a particular crystal's energy.

COLOUR-BY-CHAKRA

Different colours are thought to have their own unique qualities and represent different emotions. For example, blue is associated with perception, harmony and truth, and is said to connect with the "third eye" chakra. So if you want to feel serene, wear blue.

The seven main chakras act as energy focal points. If any of the chakras become "blocked", illnesses may occur, so keep them clear through meditation. When meditating, try visualizing an appropriate colour wrapping itself around your body.

A crystal's colour will give you a clue to its properties. Red is associated with courage, so carry red jasper if you need a bravery boost. Orange aids creativity and yellow instils happiness. Turn to green to balance the emotions. Blue allows clear communication, indigo helps you to tune in to your intuition and violet can increase your spiritual awareness.

TRY A CRYSTAL MEDITATION

If you are experiencing a particular imbalance or problem, look up the relevant crystal/chakra to focus on (or use one for each chakra and perform a general balancing meditation). Lie down comfortably and place your crystal over, or next to, the corresponding chakra. Take some slow breaths and then visualize coloured healing energy emanating from the crystal and flowing through your body. (Work from the root chakra up if you are balancing all the chakras.)

Be the energy
you want others
to absorb.

A. D. Posey

A turquoise given by a
loving hand carries with it
happiness and good fortune.

Arabic proverb

MEDITATION

The word "meditation" comes from the Latin meditari (to think, dwell on, exercise the mind) and mederi (to heal). At its simplest, meditation involves taking time out to sit still, away from distractions, and clear the mind of everyday thoughts. It allows us to take a break from "doing" and to spend time simply "being" instead, giving our minds a rest and a chance to recover from the rigours of everyday life.

Meditation forms an integral part of many ancient spiritual practices, but it is as relevant to us today as it has ever been. The benefits are enormous: on the physical side, it lowers blood pressure and boosts the immune system, while on the emotional side, it helps us to combat stress. Setting aside time to meditate also allows us to nurture our spirituality.

Anyone can learn to meditate. Start small: find a quiet place to sit for a few minutes, minimize any distractions and focus on your breathing. With practice you'll find it easier to meditate for longer periods of time.

If the idea of sitting in complete silence seems a little off-putting at first, try a guided meditation: an audio track that will talk you through a simple visualization. (This is perfect if you're new to meditating.) Some guided meditations will even help you to explore a specific issue, such as stress management or building self-confidence.

THE MIND CAN
GO IN A THOUSAND
DIRECTIONS, BUT ON
THIS BEAUTIFUL PATH,
I WALK IN PEACE.

Thích Nhất Hạnh

IF YOU CAN ATTAIN
REPOSE AND CALM,
BELIEVE THAT
YOU HAVE SEIZED
HAPPINESS.

Julie-Jeanne-Éléonore de Lespinasse

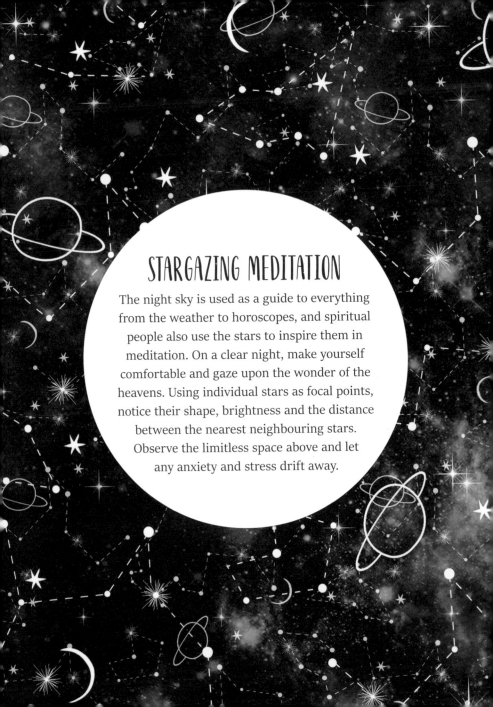

STARGAZING MEDITATION

The night sky is used as a guide to everything from the weather to horoscopes, and spiritual people also use the stars to inspire them in meditation. On a clear night, make yourself comfortable and gaze upon the wonder of the heavens. Using individual stars as focal points, notice their shape, brightness and the distance between the nearest neighbouring stars. Observe the limitless space above and let any anxiety and stress drift away.

The cosmos is within us. We are made of star-stuff. We are a way for the universe to know itself.

Carl Sagan

ESTABLISH A ROUTINE

If you can, aim to set aside 15 minutes a day to meditate. Try to meditate at the same time every day and establish a routine as you make your meditation space ready: for example, turn off your phone, close the door and arrange your cushions. This will train your brain to slow down and enter a more peaceful state of mind. Then sit quietly with your eyes closed. Focus on your breathing and the sounds around you, rather than your thoughts.

True spirituality is a mental attitude you can practise at any time.

Dalai Lama

SEEK SANCTUARY

Find a place of personal sanctuary – anything from a comfortable chair in the corner of your bedroom to a tranquil spot high upon a hill – and make time to visit it and meditate as often as you can. Away from distractions, you'll find it easier to clear your mind and nurture your spirituality.

QUIET YOUR MIND

If you find everyday thoughts clamouring for your attention – and they will at first – acknowledge them and then allow them to drift away. Remember that you have the power to control your thoughts. Don't be downhearted if you feel that a meditation session hasn't gone to plan. There is no "right" or "wrong" way to do it, and giving yourself time out is always a positive thing to do.

THOUGH YOU MAY
TRAVEL THE WORLD TO
FIND THE BEAUTIFUL,
YOU MUST HAVE IT
WITHIN YOU OR YOU
WILL FIND IT NOT.

Ralph Waldo Emerson

BREATHE DEEPLY

When we have a shock or receive bad news, we often gasp or hold our breath. This sudden, short inhalation triggers a fight-or-flight response, setting our hearts racing and making adrenalin pump around our bodies. Learn to combat this stress response with some deep, slow breaths and you'll be able to remain calm and breathe through those tricky moments.

Making time to focus on your breathing at least once a day will leave you feeling calmer. Try the humming bee breath (*brahmari*) every night before you go to bed, for example. Sit comfortably with your back straight, use the tips of your index fingers to block your ears and then inhale deeply through your nose. As you exhale through your nose, hum continuously and feel the sound vibrate through your throat and head. Repeat until you feel truly relaxed.

Real peace is unshakeable. Bliss is unchanged by gain or loss.

Yogi Bhajan

WORD POWER

Mantras and positive affirmations can help in all manner of situations, from problem-solving to stress relief. In Eastern cultures, words that are thought or vocalized are believed to have spiritual powers. It is no wonder, then, that mantras have been used in Buddhist meditation for centuries.

Find a word that inspires you when meditating and say or chant it, developing a rhythm that suits your natural breath. Affirmations are generally full sentences – "I am perfect just as I am" or "I am good enough", for example. Play around with words until you have a clutch of sentences that you can use, and alternate between them depending on your mood. Write some on sticky notes and leave them where you can see them on a daily basis to help reinforce their message.

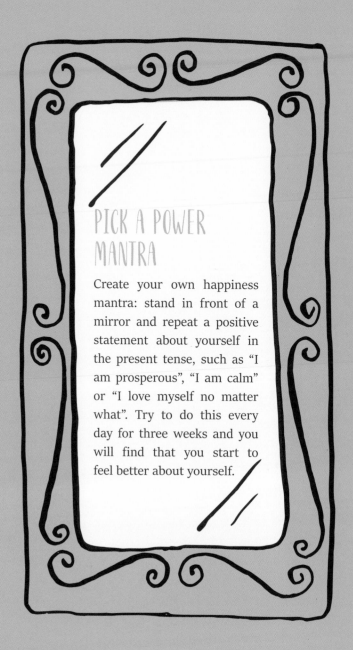

PICK A POWER MANTRA

Create your own happiness mantra: stand in front of a mirror and repeat a positive statement about yourself in the present tense, such as "I am prosperous", "I am calm" or "I love myself no matter what". Try to do this every day for three weeks and you will find that you start to feel better about yourself.

OUR SPIRITUALITY CREATES OUR WORLD BECAUSE OUR LIVES ARE A REFLECTION OF WHATEVER WE HOLD IN OUR MINDS.

David Lawrence Preston

CHANTING

Chanting – the rhythmic repetition of sounds or phrases – is a common way of connecting with the spiritual and is an integral part of many religious practices, from Buddhist throat-singing to the uplifting mantras of Hindu tradition. By focusing on chanting a simple phrase, the mind is set free from everyday thoughts and is able to reach a higher state of consciousness.

Chanting is a powerful preparation for meditation and provides us with many of the same benefits, including relaxing the mind and body, and heightening our energy and concentration levels. Chanting (or singing of any kind) allows us to release negative emotions that we may be harbouring and to avoid mental or emotional blockages.

When we chant, we are listening to the sound as well as producing it, which is why the mantras we choose can be so powerful. By repeating a simple inspirational phrase, such as "I am happy" or "All is well", we can train our minds to take a more positive approach to ourselves and to life in general.

Search online for examples of chanting and give it a try. Chanting with others certainly magnifies the benefits and an internet search will reveal any classes or chanting groups near you. You can also benefit from chanting alone, though. Use it as a tool to help you on your spiritual journey: to aid meditation, release negative emotions or reinforce positive thoughts.

To live in joy,
allow experience
to flow through
you with loving
awareness and
without clinging
or aversion.

Deepak Chopra

DISCOVER YOUR PRESSURE POINTS

Gentle pressure on points throughout the body can help us to clear blockages in our energy channels and relieve stress. If you are feeling anxious, try applying gentle pressure to the "inner gate" – a point three finger-widths down from your wrist – and you'll instantly feel more relaxed. For an energy boost, massage the webbing between your thumb and index finger of each hand. You could also look into reflexology, which can cure certain ailments, or book yourself in for a relaxing, restorative reflexology session with a professional.

YOU HAVE TO GROW FROM
THE INSIDE OUT.
NONE CAN TEACH YOU,
NONE CAN MAKE YOU
SPIRITUAL. THERE
IS NO OTHER TEACHER
BUT YOUR OWN SOUL.

Swami Vivekananda

Everything is out there
waiting for you. All you
have to do is walk up
and declare yourself in.

Stuart Wilde

SPIRITUAL HEALING

Many religious movements have a tradition of spiritual healing, although today's practitioners are often not followers of a particular faith. There are various forms of spiritual healing, but all involve the practitioner drawing on universal energy for beneficial results. This may be done through meditation, prayer or hands-on therapy in a manner similar to Reiki.

Spiritual healers are able to detect a person's aura – the multi-layered energy field that surrounds each of us. (If you've ever picked up "vibes" from someone else, you were tuning in to their aura.) Healers are highly sensitive to these energy messages and are able to learn a lot about a person's past, present and future by reading their aura. They can then go on to discuss any issues as well as directing healing energy to where it is needed.

Spiritual healing is the most widely practised alternative therapy, with many people putting their faith in the positive results it has been seen to achieve. (The NHS employs healers to help seriously ill patients.) The most important lesson we can learn from it is the power of kind thoughts and intentions. Focusing our goodwill and positivity on another individual (or ourselves) can have a huge beneficial impact. Practise every day and see the results of your compassion.

Ultimately, spiritual awareness unfolds when you're spontaneous... when you're flexible, when you're easy on yourself and easy on others.

Deepak Chopra

For attractive lips, speak words of kindness. For lovely eyes, seek out the good in people.

Sam Levenson

SEND HEALING ENERGY

We are all familiar with the feeling of comfort that a hug can bring, but we can learn to project feelings of positivity to our loved ones over many miles, too. Spiritual energy is not limited by geography, so try sending healing vibes to someone you know who needs them. Sit quietly and think about your chosen person. Consider what you admire about them, then think about what they might need – love, courage, comfort or peace – and send them those thoughts.

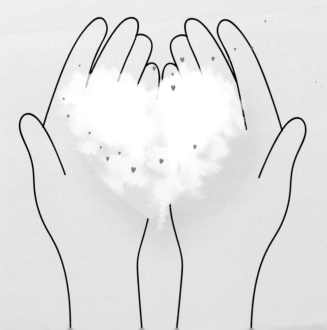

TUNE IN TO VIBES

We can all learn to be more sensitive to people's vibes and use this sensitivity to enhance our relationships. Take a moment to see what you can detect about someone's energy: are they in a good mood or feeling harassed? Are they in need of comfort? And how does your energy change when you are with them? Do you feel boosted or wary? Your physical reaction is more telling than your mind's, so tune in to that.

HAPPINESS IS WHEN

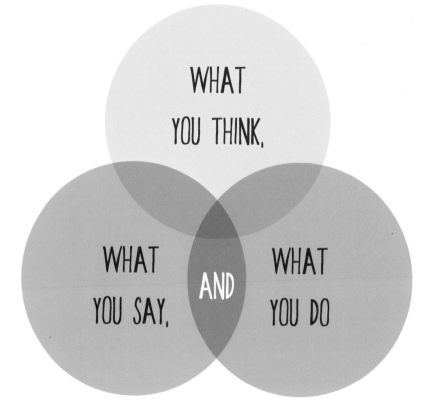

WHAT
YOU THINK,

WHAT
YOU SAY,

AND

WHAT
YOU DO

ARE IN HARMONY.

Mahatma Gandhi

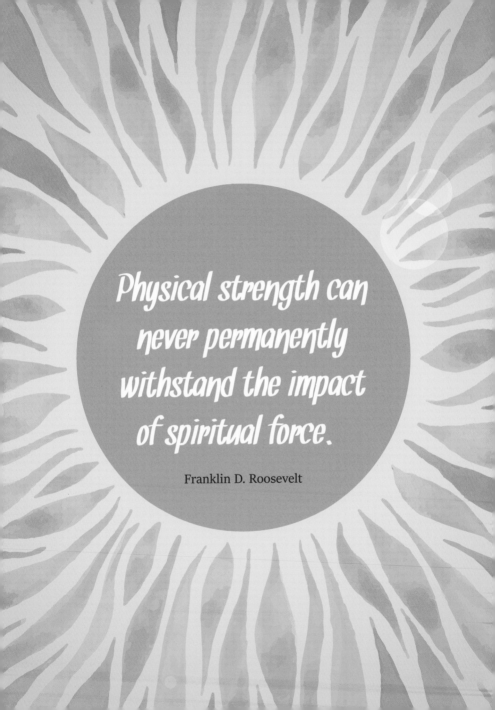

PART 3

Spiritual Development

LEARN TO CONNECT

Get into the habit of making eye contact when you speak to someone. Looking at someone properly establishes an unspoken connection that makes communication much more honest and meaningful. The person you are in conversation with is left in no doubt that you are focused on them and that you value what they are saying.

Just as eye contact helps establish a more positive connection, so too does listening properly. Practise giving people your full attention when you are in one-to-one conversations; watch how often you interrupt them with your own point of view or attempt to shout them down. By truly listening empathetically we are acknowledging the importance of another person. We also allow ourselves to hear something interesting that may even change our viewpoint. Keep your eyes and ears open and your heart and mind will follow.

The face is a picture of the mind
as the eyes are its interpreter.

Marcus Tullius Cicero

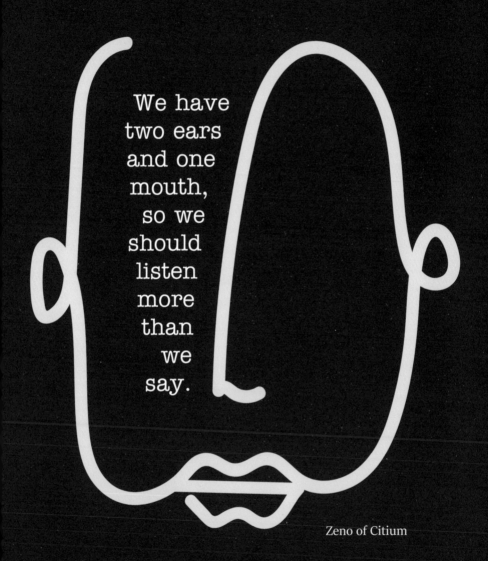

We have
two ears
and one
mouth,
so we
should
listen
more
than
we
say.

Zeno of Citium

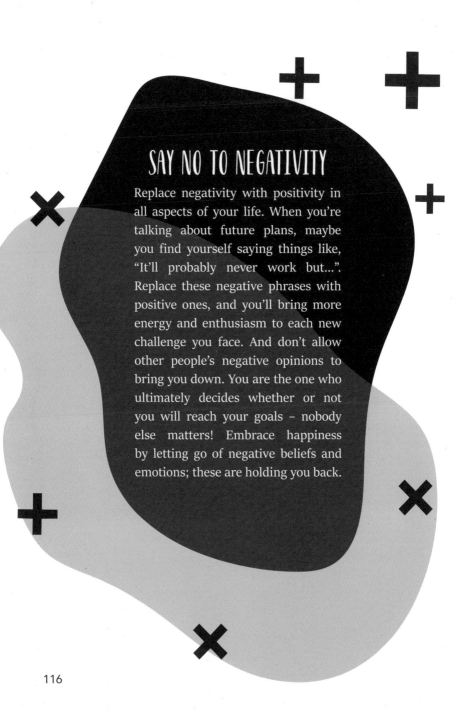

SAY NO TO NEGATIVITY

Replace negativity with positivity in all aspects of your life. When you're talking about future plans, maybe you find yourself saying things like, "It'll probably never work but...". Replace these negative phrases with positive ones, and you'll bring more energy and enthusiasm to each new challenge you face. And don't allow other people's negative opinions to bring you down. You are the one who ultimately decides whether or not you will reach your goals – nobody else matters! Embrace happiness by letting go of negative beliefs and emotions; these are holding you back.

Some people
grumble that roses
have thorns:
I am grateful that
thorns have roses.

Jean-Baptiste Alphonse Karr

HAVE A GRATITUDE ATTITUDE

What makes you feel grateful in your life? Take regular stock of all you have to be grateful for, and of the things that make you feel better or happy – those things that give you a warm feeling inside. From the clothes on your back to the roof over your head, count all your blessings, including those we often take for granted. Start a physical gratitude list. Add to it over the course of a year and then look back at all that you have to be thankful for.

Alternatively, create a mental gratitude list at the end of each day, as you are preparing to sleep. Go through the day and recognize all that you had, did and encountered that deserves a "thank you". Both spirituality and sleep come far easier when you have a full and appreciative heart.

If the only prayer
you ever said was
thank you, that
would be enough.

Meister Eckhart

TO ERR IS HUMAN; TO FORGIVE, DIVINE

It is difficult – virtually impossible – to bring a more spiritual approach into your life when you feel angry, defensive, bitter or awash with resentment against another person. Nursing resentment is both damaging and thought-muddling. Ancient wisdom and modern-day clinical trials concur that forgiveness brings health benefits. Acts of forgiveness, while often difficult, can yield substantial rewards such as improved relationships, reduced anxiety, better heart health, a more robust immune system and lower stress levels and blood pressure.

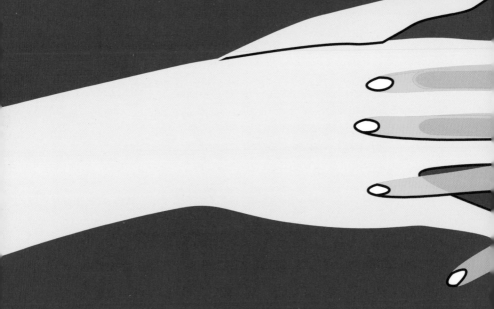

Most importantly, forgiveness brings peace of mind. Letting go of resentment is good for clearing our spiritual pathways, and shouldn't be underestimated. Holding on to bitterness inspires negativity and makes it impossible to achieve a state of repose. The past is not there to be dwelt upon, so forgive others even when they don't deserve it: you deserve the peace.

Forgive. Acknowledge the hurt, remember to never treat anyone that way, and move on with grace and purpose.

Forgiveness is not an occasional act — it is a constant attitude.

Martin Luther King Jr

BE YOUR OWN HAPPY MAGNET

To attract joy, become your own happy magnet. The laws of attraction say that if you want to feel happier, pull happiness towards you. Try seeking out those who inspire happy feelings, doing something that you know always lifts your heart, or, simply, looking on that which makes you smile. Whether it is watching your favourite stand-up comedian or gazing into the eyes of a loved one, live your happiness in every way that you can.

When your mood isn't especially upbeat, try faking it. There is some evidence to suggest that people who start the day in a despondent frame of mind but who make a conscious effort to act as if they were happy can actually lift their mood and alter their sense of spiritual well-being significantly. Happiness is also contagious, so try passing it on!

When you do
things from
your soul,

you feel a river
moving in you,
a joy.

Rumi

SPREAD A LITTLE HAPPINESS

A small act of kindness goes a long way. To be kind is to consider someone else and their needs. To offer kindness to a stranger or to someone we don't particularly like is to touch a soul. There are countless (pleasantly surprising) benefits of extending kindness – from the developing of new friendships to the returning of favours. The greatest reward, however, is the sense of humanity and purpose that selfless giving brings.

Look for daily opportunities to be kind, whether it's just a small act or giving time, skills or money. Volunteer, donate old clothes and goods to someone who would benefit from the gift, or reach out to someone going through a hard time. Better still, become a kindness ninja! Perform an act of kindness so secretly and swiftly that the recipient has no idea who their benefactor was. Put your spare change in a vending machine as a surprise for the next person who wants to use it, or wash up any dirty mugs or dishes in your workplace kitchen. The feel-good effects of being kind are life-affirming.

A SINGLE ACT OF KINDNESS THROWS OUT ROOTS IN ALL DIRECTIONS, AND THE ROOTS SPRING UP AND MAKE NEW TREES.

Amelia Earhart

Go into the
world and
do well.
But more
importantly,
go into the
world and
do good.

Minor Myers Jr

DON'T WASTE YOUR WORDS

It's all too easy to get drawn in to listening to unpleasant talk about others, but words – like actions – have consequences, and lending your ear to this sort of negativity can only be a bad thing. Words are a wonderful tool for spreading joy and happiness so avoid wasting them. Choose to pay someone a compliment instead. You'll both feel the benefits.

*Words are also seeds,
and when dropped into the
invisible spiritual substance,
they grow and bring forth
after their kind.*

Charles Fillmore

A man is but the
product of his thoughts.
What he thinks,
he becomes.

Mahatma Gandhi

PONDER YOUR PURPOSE

The spiritual journey is an intensely personal one. Find a quiet moment and look within yourself to discover what it really is that you want from life. Ask yourself what your purpose is. If you find you don't know what your purpose is, that's OK. Try asking different questions, about your talents, passions and how you like to spend your free time; you may find the answers point in a certain direction.

When we strip away life's excesses and distractions, it becomes easier to focus on our true priorities. Find these, and focus your energy and intentions on them.

The meaning of life is to find your gift. The purpose of life is to give it away.

Pablo Picasso

Three things in human
life are important:

the first is to
BE KIND;

the second is to
BE KIND;

and the third is to
BE KIND.

Henry James

KARMA

The idea that our every action has consequences (either in this life or the next) is familiar to us through expressions such as: "You reap what you sow." Karma is central to many ancient belief systems. Buddhism, Hinduism, Sikhism and Jainism all emphasize the importance of the karmic principle: good deeds will lead to happy consequences; bad deeds will cause us future suffering.

Many religions are built around the belief that the soul moves on to a new body after death – and so the sins of past lives may be carried forward, resulting in negative experiences in the present (and future). These traditions teach that past lives can affect the family a person is surrounded by, as well as their self-belief and even their health.

Whether you believe in reincarnation or not, it's certainly the case that a person who does good deeds is more likely to trigger a positive reaction in others than a person who does not. Scientific studies prove that showing compassion affects the hormones that are released into our bloodstream: thoughts of kindness produce oxytocin, which makes us more trusting, less anxious and more receptive to the emotions of others. By actively choosing to behave in a kind manner, we will feel happier and be better equipped to build strong relationships. Repeatedly behaving in this way will change our neural pathways, too, and make us more likely to repeat that type of behaviour in the future. By being kind, we become better people.

READ A SPIRITUAL BOOK

Thinking about spirituality might not be something we do regularly, and might even feel uncomfortable at first, but we shouldn't let that put us off trying to connect with something fundamental that is within all of us. To get you thinking about spiritual matters, explore the Mind, Body and Spirit section of your local bookshop and see if a title jumps out at you. Whether you agree with what you read or not, it will be a good starting point.

GIVE SOMETHING BACK

Charitable endeavour, like faith, gives meaning to our lives and is a truly reliable source of joy. There are so many ways you can give something back to your community. You're bound to be able to find something that appeals to you, whether it's working for a wildlife charity, helping at a youth group or taking time to chat to someone who is housebound. Visit www.do-it.org to find dozens of opportunities to help others near you.

FIND THE MIDDLE WAY

The Buddha taught that neither a life of luxury nor one of austerity would aid spiritual development and bring happiness. He recommended following a balanced lifestyle – the Middle Way – in which individuals develop the discipline to live an ethical life. A balanced approach can be beneficial in many areas of our lives, so strive to cultivate discipline and avoid over-indulging, but do not deny yourself life's pleasures either.

DON'T DWELL ON PAINFUL EXPERIENCES

We all encounter difficult situations in life. The pain of the experience itself is upsetting enough, but many of us tend to relive upsetting moments time and again, prolonging our discomfort, in a reaction that Buddhists call the second arrow of suffering. Remember that while we may be unable to control what happens in life, we can control our thoughts. Resolve not to dwell on difficult situations and avoid the pain of the second arrow.

As we cultivate peace and
happiness in ourselves,
we also nourish peace and
happiness in those we love.

Thích Nhất Hạnh

NURTURE UNCONDITIONAL LOVE

When you follow your spiritual path, try to tune in to feelings of unconditional love for others and yourself. Change negative aspects into positive ones, even when you need to summon up inner strength to do this. You may find that meditating or practising mindfulness will help you to detach from any negative reactions that you are experiencing. Cultivate a feeling of loving kindness and acceptance instead, and remember to draw on this in challenging times.

CLEAR THE AIR

Our relationships will never reach their true potential if we are weighed down by past disagreements or misunderstandings. If a relationship is worth nurturing, make the effort to clear the air, talk through any unresolved issues, and agree to leave these in the past. Move forward, free of grudges and resentment, and enjoy the positive energy of a refreshed relationship lived fully in the present moment.

ANGER
BEGETS MORE
ANGER, AND
FORGIVENESS
AND LOVE
LEAD TO MORE
FORGIVENESS
AND LOVE.

Mahavira

WE HAVE
FORGOTTEN
HOW TO BE GOOD
GUESTS, HOW
TO WALK LIGHTLY
ON THE EARTH
AS ITS OTHER
CREATURES DO.

Barbara Ward

MAKE ECO-FRIENDLY CHOICES

Consider the impact of our lives on other living creatures and the world around us. While veganism may not be for you, you might decide to look into where the food you buy is sourced and make different choices accordingly. Are there other ways in which you could soften your impact on the planet? When we consider our relationship with other living things, we learn to value all life more, including our own.

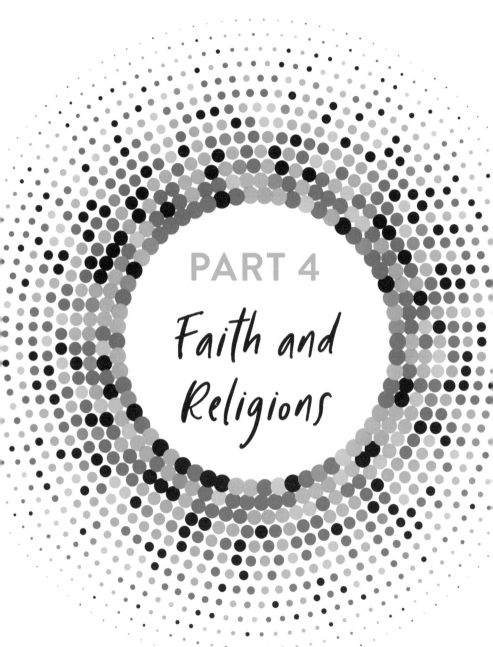

PART 4

Faith and Religions

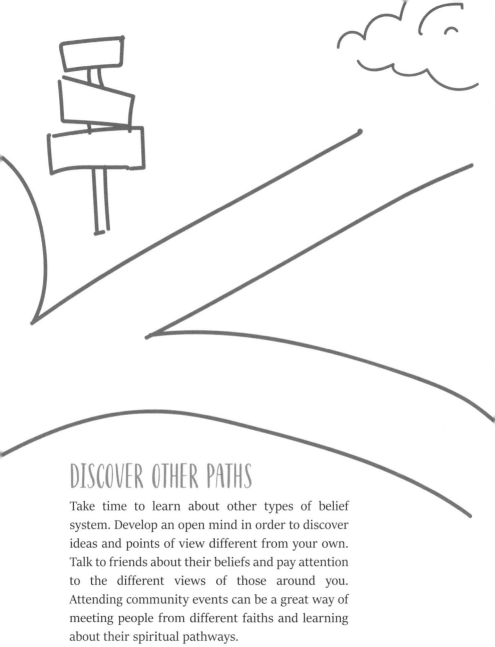

DISCOVER OTHER PATHS

Take time to learn about other types of belief system. Develop an open mind in order to discover ideas and points of view different from your own. Talk to friends about their beliefs and pay attention to the different views of those around you. Attending community events can be a great way of meeting people from different faiths and learning about their spiritual pathways.

THEOSOPHY

Meaning "wisdom of the gods", theosophy refers to hidden knowledge or mystical insight that offers enlightenment and salvation. Theosophists believe that this knowledge lies at the heart of every religion, with different spiritual beliefs providing different pathways to the same wisdom. Theosophists use discussion, research and meditation to seek this wisdom out.

In antiquity, theosophy existed in various forms, but the modern movement was set up in the United States in the late nineteenth century. Individuals decide on their own principles to live by, which often reflect the beliefs at the heart of the movement: that all life is one entity (so by helping others we are helping ourselves); that life and death are part of a continuous cycle; and that the purpose of life is to learn. Theosophists respect nature and the environment, and may choose to be vegetarian. They often actively support human rights movements and strive for all forms of equality.

As theosophy draws together all religions (along with science and philosophy), humanity is regarded as part of a single spiritual family and theosophy teaches us to approach others with compassion and understanding, even when their views may seem very different from our own.

By having a reverence for life, we enter into a spiritual relation with the world.

Albert Schweitzer

MODERN PAGANISM

Paganism in general refers to the religious traditions of a country's indigenous population and is an umbrella term for many ancient spiritual beliefs, but in the West paganism refers to a more specific spiritual path. Modern pagans, such as Druids or Wiccans, share a deep reverence for nature, and an understanding that all life is connected and should be respected. Many also choose to follow an eco-friendly lifestyle.

Modern pagans observe the cycle of the seasons, the moon and life itself (from birth to death), and eight annual festivals are celebrated throughout the year. These mark the "turn of the wheel" and tie in to the natural cycles of the planet. They include the equinoxes, solstices and four additional seasonal festivals. Pagans feel that our lives can be lived in harmony with these changes; for example, that it is beneficial to plan new projects in the spring.

For pagans, connecting with nature is an important part of their spiritual practice in a world where many of us feel that we've lost that natural connection. We spend our time in centrally heated buildings and tend to follow the same daily routine week in, week out. Studies have shown the benefits of spending time in nature, so incorporating elements of a pagan outlook into our lives can have a huge positive impact on our mental and physical well-being.

ENGAGE WITH NATURE

Pagans use the different elements – earth, water, air and fire – to enhance various characteristics in their lives. If you feel unsettled, try grounding yourself by walking barefoot on grass or sand. To release pent-up emotions, soak in a warm bath or spend time near water. Sharpen your thinking by getting out and about on a blustery day and breathing in the fresh air. Use candlelight and fire to help your intuition and passions to burn more brightly.

Connect with the cycle of the seasons by making a fresh start in the spring and sow the seeds of new projects for the year ahead. Soak in the warmth of the sun's rays in the summer and re-energize. At harvest time, give thanks for the good things in your life. And as the trees lose their leaves in autumn and winter, take stock of your life and shed any possessions or habits that are no longer useful to you.

THE TURN OF THE WHEEL

Paganism recognizes the cyclical nature of life: out of every ending comes a new beginning. In order to move forward, we have to learn to let go of the past. The world is ever changing, the wheel ever turning – just as dawn follows the darkest hour of night, happier times follow on from those of trial and difficulty. Learn to be patient and remember: dark times will pass and make way for bright, new beginnings.

Trying to understand is like straining through muddy water. Have the patience to wait! Be still and allow the mud to settle.

Lao Tzu

SHAMANISM

Shamanism is often associated with Native American culture, but shamanic practices have existed in indigenous populations the world over for centuries. They all have one key belief at their core: everything in nature has a spirit and wisdom to share. Shamanism involves tapping into this universal wisdom – often through "journeying" – to heal individuals at a spiritual level. During journeying, the shamanic healer will use drumming or singing to enter an altered state and access an other-worldly dimension where they can receive wisdom from past ancestors or animal guides.

Shamanic healing can also involve "soul retrieval". Practitioners believe that when we experience shocking events, we lose fragments of our soul, or we may give fragments away during intense relationships. Journeying allows a healer to help a person to retrieve these fragments and recover from past traumas.

As it is rooted in the ancient cultures of indigenous people, shamanic wisdom helps us to connect with our ancestors when we incorporate it into our everyday lives. Its basic principles are to embrace nature; to heal the environment, others and oneself; and to set aside time to journey (or meditate) regularly and work on unifying the mind, body and spirit. Many shamanic teachers offer introductory workshops where people can discover more about shamanism and even learn to journey.

RELAXING RHYTHMS

Shamanic healers often use drums or rattles to enter the meditative state needed for journeying. Listening to a repeated tempo of between four and seven beats per second will cause the brain to enter a theta-wave state. (We all experience this during light sleep and many people achieve it during deep meditation.) If you find meditating a challenge, it could be worth listening to shamanic drumming online – or even investing in your own drum or rattle.

SEEING YOUR SPIRIT ANIMAL

Shamans work with animal guides and believe
that all of us have power animals beside us in
a spiritual form. We attract different guides at
different stages of our lives, so your spirit animal
may change. Pay attention to any creatures that
crop up in dreams or that you find yourself
drawn to in books, to discover your companion
and their symbolism or relevance to you.

If you realized how powerful your thoughts are, you would never think a negative thought.

Peace Pilgrim

TIME FOR TAO

Taoism as a discipline has its origins in ancient China: Lao Tzu, a prominent sage of the sixth century BCE, is credited as its founder. Tao is loosely translated as "the way", and this spiritual tradition is based on the belief that there is a single all-pervading energy, known as chi, guiding everything along its path. True tao cannot be articulated, but felt only by becoming attuned to nature and achieving harmony with the rhythms of the universe.

The objective of Taoism is to experience life in an effortless way and therefore to keep energy flowing when you need it. An important principle is "action through inaction". Known as wu wei, this involves understanding the flow of energy around you and therefore the optimum time for action – when to act and when to relax. In your everyday life, carefully consider the moments when not acting on a thought or feeling may be more beneficial to you in the long run.

THE MOON DOES NOT FIGHT.
IT ATTACKS NO ONE. IT DOES
NOT WORRY. IT DOES NOT
TRY TO CRUSH OTHERS.

Deng Ming-Dao

BUDDHISM

Buddhists pursue the spiritual state of enlightenment through practices such as meditation, reflection and rituals. They follow the path of the Buddha, Siddhartha Gautama, who began his own quest for enlightenment some time in the sixth or fifth century BCE. Buddhism is best seen as a philosophy rather than a religion, as Buddhists do not worship deities.

Buddhism teaches that nothing is fixed, and that change is always possible. Its major insight is that human suffering is caused by our belief that things will last and our craving for things to be a certain way. Only when we let go of such cravings can we truly be happy.

In practical terms, Buddhism is a flexible belief system that may be applied to everyday life. Although it is an ancient philosophy, it has much to offer in a modern world where speed, achievement and conspicuous consumption are highly prized. If you're interested in learning more about Buddhism, pay a visit to your local meditation centre or pick up a book on its teachings to see if it's right for you.

Thousands of candles can
be lighted from a single
candle, and the life of the
candle will not be shortened.
Happiness never decreases
by being shared.

Buddhist proverb

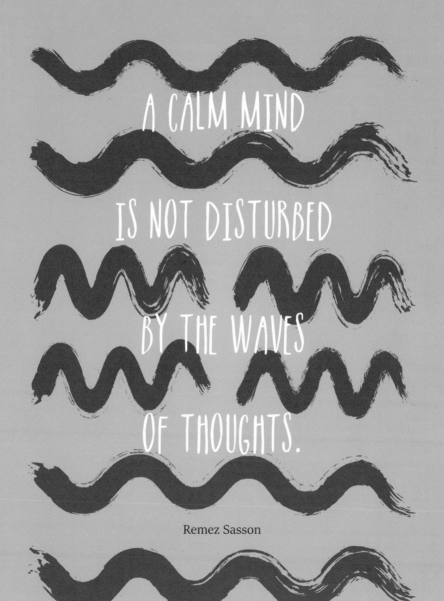

A CALM MIND

IS NOT DISTURBED

BY THE WAVES

OF THOUGHTS.

Remez Sasson

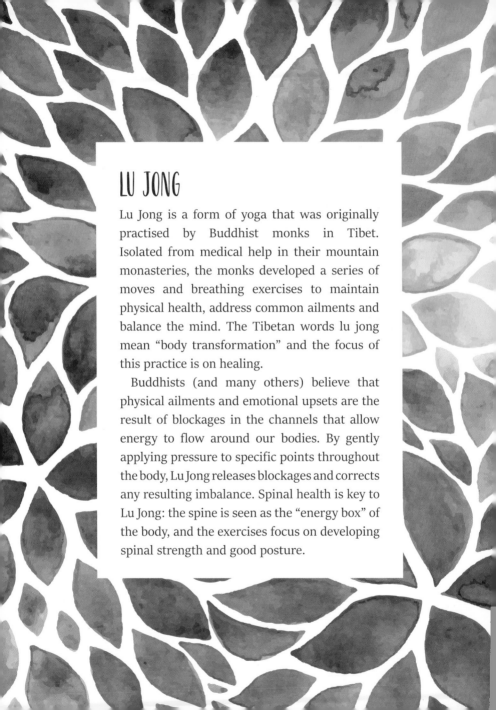

LU JONG

Lu Jong is a form of yoga that was originally practised by Buddhist monks in Tibet. Isolated from medical help in their mountain monasteries, the monks developed a series of moves and breathing exercises to maintain physical health, address common ailments and balance the mind. The Tibetan words lu jong mean "body transformation" and the focus of this practice is on healing.

Buddhists (and many others) believe that physical ailments and emotional upsets are the result of blockages in the channels that allow energy to flow around our bodies. By gently applying pressure to specific points throughout the body, Lu Jong releases blockages and corrects any resulting imbalance. Spinal health is key to Lu Jong: the spine is seen as the "energy box" of the body, and the exercises focus on developing spinal strength and good posture.

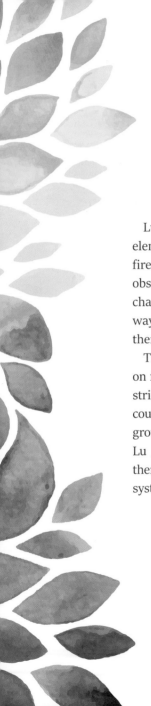

Lu Jong is based on balancing the five elements of the universe – space, earth, wind, fire and water – within the body. Tibetan monks observed that the balance of these elements changes throughout the day and identified ways in which we can work in harmony with them at these times.

The four groups of Lu Jong movements flow on from one another and should be practised in strict order. The best place to start is a beginners' course, which will introduce you to the first group of moves – the Five Elements. Although Lu Jong classes may be tricky to track down, there are some great online resources about this system of Tibetan medicine and philosophy.

If I keep a green bough in my heart then the singing bird will come.

Chinese proverb

T'AI CHI

The origins of this graceful martial art are shrouded in mystery, although it is believed to have originated in thirteenth-century China. T'ai chi as we know it today can be traced back to the Chen region, and Chen style t'ai chi remains one of the most popular forms.

The practice combines solo routines with breathing and meditation exercises, alongside response drills and self-defence manoeuvres. There are several different schools of t'ai chi, some of which are more challenging than others. In addition, some classes blend characteristics of the different schools, but this diversity means that it's easy to find a class to suit you. T'ai chi is extremely popular and there is a wealth of information for the beginner to tap in to, both online and in the form of books, DVDs and courses.

The principle of yin and yang lies at the heart of this practice and is characterized in the t'ai chi symbol, which represents the balance of opposite forces in the universe and its continuous movement around a central point of stillness and calm. T'ai chi students learn to harness and balance their own energy, and to find clarity of mind while focusing on the flow of slow and deliberate movements. As with other holistic practices, it benefits students on a physical, emotional and spiritual level, and it has often been called meditation in motion.

With the gentlest movements of t'ai chi comes the quieting of emotions.

Justin Stone

T'ai chi... is the wisdom of your own senses, your own mind and body together as one process.

Chungliang Al Huang

TAKE A MEASURED APPROACH

In t'ai chi, students learn to use just enough strength to carry out each move – not too much and not too little – and so they achieve perfect balance. We can use this principle in many areas of our lives: in reacting appropriately to others, for instance. We can use enough strength to stand up for ourselves without being aggressive, but not too little or we become weak. We can learn to be firm but flexible, strong but loving.

FIND UNITY IN DIVERSITY

The t'ai chi symbol reminds us that everything in creation is formed of a balance of opposites: we are all created the same and are part of a greater whole. When you encounter challenging people, remind yourself that no one is essentially good or bad: we are all humans, doing our best to cope with life's twists and turns. You cannot know what turmoil others may be facing, so try to cultivate a loving and kind attitude to others – and to yourself.

QIGONG

Qigong is a system of movement and meditation that focuses on balancing the body's chi, or essential energy, to benefit body and mind. It has its roots in ancient Chinese culture and qigong translates as "energy cultivation". The system combines slow sequences of moves with breathing exercises and positive visualizations to explore the connection between mind, body and spirit.

Qigong is practised by millions of people the world over and many different forms have developed. Some are more dynamic – it can be used as martial arts training, for example – while others focus on static postures for healing particular ailments or meditative poses for spiritual development. (The health benefits of qigong are such that it is included on the syllabus of many medical schools in China.)

As there is such a variety of qigong styles, anyone can find a version to suit them, whatever their age or lifestyle. Whether you are seeking stress release, improved fitness or increased self-awareness, there's a form of qigong for you. The internet is a wonderful tool for finding out more about qigong, and there are numerous books, DVDs and classes available too.

Whatever style you choose, qigong allows you to reconnect with your spirit. At its heart are three simple principles: correct your posture, deepen your breathing and open your mind. If you aim to do these three things when you have a quiet moment, you'll be putting a little knowledge from this centuries-old system to good use.

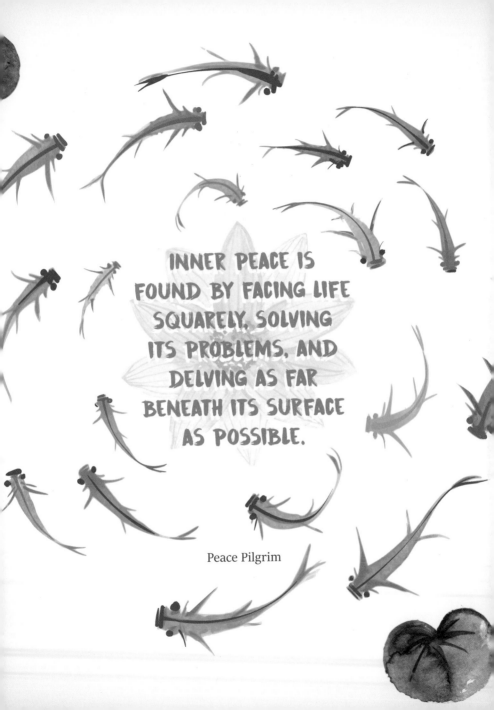

INNER PEACE IS
FOUND BY FACING LIFE
SQUARELY, SOLVING
ITS PROBLEMS, AND
DELVING AS FAR
BENEATH ITS SURFACE
AS POSSIBLE.

Peace Pilgrim

The moment one gives
close attention
to anything...
it becomes a
mysterious, awesome,
indescribably
magnificent
world in itself.

Henry Miller

TRY AIKIDO

Aikido, a Japanese martial art – "the art of peace" – harmonizes mind and movement, allowing students to defend themselves by deflecting the energy of their attacker. It was developed by Morihei Ueshiba in the 1920s, and is a blend of his knowledge of jujitsu with sword and staff skills and his own defensive moves. Aikido teaches practitioners to find a place of calm during stressful circumstances.

A quest for peace and harmony is essential to the philosophy of aikido and this spiritual element was outlined in Ueshiba's writings. He explained that the correct mindset for a student is not to seek victory over their opponent, but to seek peace with the universe: "True budo [martial arts practice] is the loving protection of all beings with a spirit of reconciliation." Aikido moves typically involve either joint immobilization or throws using the opponent's momentum.

Like t'ai chi, aikido is a popular activity and finding a local class should not be too challenging. As well as helping you learn defensive skills, gain confidence and improve your reflexes, aikido offers a spiritual dimension in which you can pursue inner peace and learn to take a step back from conflict. Aikido teaches us that meeting violence with violence is not the best way forward. It shows us the importance of acting rather than reacting and can help us to take control of the challenges we encounter in day-to-day life.

HINDUISM

Often regarded as the world's oldest religion, Hinduism is actually an umbrella term for a collection of spiritual, philosophical and cultural ideas characterized by the law of karma and the idea of the immortality of the soul. Hinduism has its roots in the Vedic traditions that developed in India over three thousand years ago. With its long history, Hinduism has absorbed many religious beliefs over time and tolerance is an important part of its approach.

Three deities are central to Hinduism: Brahma (the supreme creator), Vishnu (the preserver) and Shiva (the destroyer). In addition to these, Hindus are free to choose which deities they worship, and many local gods and goddesses may be acknowledged in their daily rituals. (Yoga is often used as a way to still the mind and gain spiritual insight.)

Broadly, Hinduism outlines four goals in life: to live by an agreed moral code, to lawfully pursue material gain, to understand and respect the concept of karma, and – ultimately – to aim for the soul to be released from the constant cycle of rebirth (to achieve *moksha*). An individual can achieve moksha through a life of hard work, selfless actions and devotion to their chosen deities.

Another important aspect of contemporary Hinduism is the pursuit of justice through non-violent means, as exemplified by Mahatma Gandhi. His philosophy of non-violence encourages us to love all and hate no one.

MY WISDOM FLOWS FROM THE HIGHEST
SOURCE. I SALUTE THAT SOURCE IN YOU. LET
US WORK TOGETHER FOR UNITY AND LOVE.

Mahatma Gandhi

Our greatest glory is not in never falling, but in rising every time we fall.

Confucius

JAINISM

Jainism is an ancient Indian belief system that was shaped into its present form by Mahavira, a religious reformer born in 599 BCE, whom Jains believe to be the latest in a line of spiritual teachers. There are no gods in Jainism; the goal of spiritual life is to achieve release from the cycle of reincarnation by freeing the soul from all karma (good or bad). Full responsibility for achieving this falls on individuals and how they conduct themselves.

Followers strive to live a life of self-denial and achieve five key principles: chastity, no lying, no stealing, non-attachment and non-violence. The latter is most important and – as Jains believe that all living things have souls – it extends to all creatures, not just fellow human beings. Followers are strict vegetarians and choose to live in the most eco-friendly way possible.

Meditation is an important part of daily spiritual practice and Jains follow the Path of the Three Jewels in order to embody the key principles of their religion. These jewels are: right conduct, right faith and right knowledge. Atonement for sins is another key principle; individuals must confess their sins from the past year to family and friends at the annual Paryushana festival, when all pledge to move forward without bearing grudges.

CONFUCIANISM

The teachings of the Chinese philosopher Kong Qiu – or Confucius, as he is known in the West – date from the sixth century BCE. Confucius believed that all humans are perfectible through self-cultivation and that by living in an ethical manner we can achieve a state of benevolence known as res. Confucius felt that this wisdom was not handed down by the gods, but already existed in human hearts and minds. He emphasized the importance of learning from the past and putting this knowledge into practice in everyday life.

As well as outlining the principles we should live by to achieve res, including sincerity, honesty, modesty and kindness, Confucius considered the qualities we should cultivate in our relationships with others – as parents, children, siblings and friends, for example. He gave great weight to the importance of embracing our roles in life and carrying them out in the appropriate manner.

Though not overtly spiritual with regard to focusing on the elusive or ethereal, Confucianism asserts that by achieving res and enacting this in our everyday lives, we can forge a stronger connection with our spiritual side and realize our full potential.

CULTIVATE RES

The five constant virtues of Confucianism, which we should strive to uphold in our everyday behaviour, are: honesty, modesty, kindness, diligence and sincerity. Together these qualities embody res ("goodness"). Consider what these qualities mean to you. When was the last time you noticed these attributes in others? Do you embody these virtues in your day-to-day life or is there, perhaps, one that you could try to cultivate more often or more fully?

To be wronged is nothing unless you continue to remember it.

Confucius

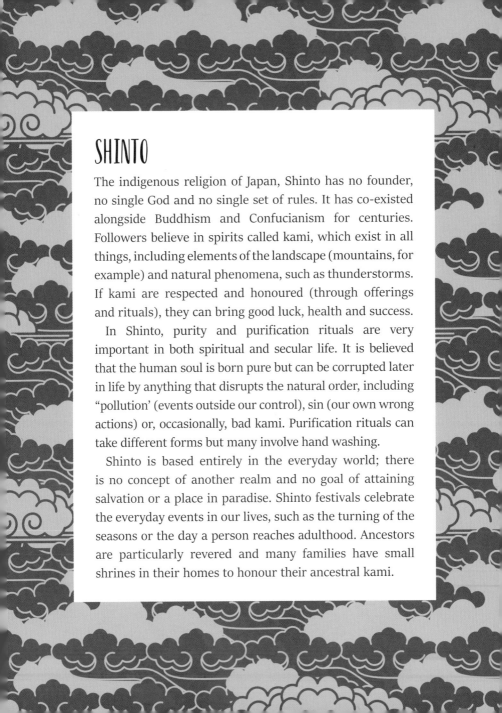

SHINTO

The indigenous religion of Japan, Shinto has no founder, no single God and no single set of rules. It has co-existed alongside Buddhism and Confucianism for centuries. Followers believe in spirits called kami, which exist in all things, including elements of the landscape (mountains, for example) and natural phenomena, such as thunderstorms. If kami are respected and honoured (through offerings and rituals), they can bring good luck, health and success.

In Shinto, purity and purification rituals are very important in both spiritual and secular life. It is believed that the human soul is born pure but can be corrupted later in life by anything that disrupts the natural order, including "pollution' (events outside our control), sin (our own wrong actions) or, occasionally, bad kami. Purification rituals can take different forms but many involve hand washing.

Shinto is based entirely in the everyday world; there is no concept of another realm and no goal of attaining salvation or a place in paradise. Shinto festivals celebrate the everyday events in our lives, such as the turning of the seasons or the day a person reaches adulthood. Ancestors are particularly revered and many families have small shrines in their homes to honour their ancestral kami.

TAKE A PURIFYING BATH

Shinto rituals use water or salt for purification, and the cleansing power of a salt bath is recommended by many for purifying not only the body (salt water draws toxins out of your tissues), but your aura too. Treat yourself to a ritual cleansing bath once a month. Use warm water (not too hot) with a couple of handfuls of unprocessed salt such as Himalayan rock salt. Light candles, play soothing music and wash away any negative thoughts.

SIKHISM

Sikhism, based on the teachings of Guru Nanak (1469–1539) and his nine followers, originated in the Punjab. Nanak felt that the rituals of other religions detracted from the pursuit of a relationship with God. He taught that actively doing good works – rather than carrying out rituals – was the most effective way of showing devotion to God.

Sikhs believe that humans cannot hope to understand God, but they can use ordinary life to get close to him, and can experience him through worship and contemplation. (Sikhism teaches that there is only one God for all religions.) By focusing on God in this way, Sikhs believe that they will ultimately be freed from the cycle of reincarnation.

Today, the emphasis of Sikhism is still very much on actively carrying out good works and benefitting the community, while keeping God in mind at all times. Sikhism has long been linked with a commitment to justice, and followers are taught to defend the defenceless and stand up to oppression.

A Sikh is expected to live honestly, be generous and treat others equally. The Sikh place of worship (the Gurdwara) is open to people of all faiths and is often the centre of the community. Decisions are made by the Sikh community as a group – there are no clergy – and men and women have equal status, making Sikhism a particularly egalitarian religion.

BAHÁ'Í

This relatively new religion was established in Iran in 1863 by Bahá'u'lláh. Followers believe in unity, the equality of men and women, and the importance of working together for the common good. They believe that humans are all part of the same family and that only by transforming ourselves can we tackle the issues of society as a whole, such as economic problems, the need for world peace and the eradication of prejudice.

Bahá'í teachings state that God reveals himself in stages and that the gods of all other religions, which they also accept and respect, are part of this gradual revelation process. (Bahá'u'lláh is seen as the latest in the line of revelations, but not the last.)

There are no clergy in the Bahá'í faith, but it is a spiritual path that must be walked in the company of others, who can encourage and advise as they travel together. The importance of family and of helping the wider community as a whole are also emphasized. Bahá'ís believe that they should work daily to improve themselves and that in doing so they are working towards the betterment of society – a principle that can inspire anyone on their spiritual journey.

When you are kind to others it not only changes you, it also changes the world.

Harold Kushner

Ye are the fruits of one tree, and the leaves of one branch.

Bahá'u'lláh

REFLECT WITHIN AND WITHOUT

There may be challenges to overcome as you examine your spirituality. You may feel confused as you question beliefs and start to feel differently about some aspects of the world around you – re-evaluating a tricky relationship or pondering the implications of a problem at work, for example. Spirituality teaches us that reflecting on the outer world helps us to reflect on our inner landscape. As your sense of spirituality grows, you will find inner peace more easily.

Let your vision be world-embracing rather than confined to your own self.

Bahá'u'lláh

CONCLUSION

No two roads toward spiritual enlightenment are the same, but all are equally valid. We hope this book has inspired you to try out some of the life-changing practices and belief systems at your disposal, and will lead you to look further into the ones that speak to you most, in order to continue your spiritual education. Wherever your journey takes you – whether you find comfort in chakras, wisdom in Buddhism or peace in t'ai chi – we wish you well, and may you find peace, positivity and happiness in your new, spiritual life.

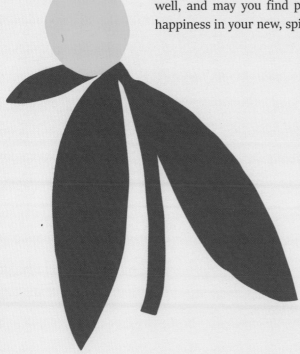

If you're interested in finding out more about our books,
find us on Facebook at **Summersdale Publishers**
and follow us on Twitter at **@Summersdale**.

www.summersdale.com

Image credits